TIBET

Bobbie Kalman

The Lands, Peoples, and Cultures Series

Crabtree Publishing Company

The Lands, Peoples, and Cultures Series
Created by Bobbie Kalman

Written by
Christine Arthurs
Margaret Hoogeveen

Editor-in-Chief
Bobbie Kalman

Editors
Margaret Hoogeveen
Christine Arthurs

Design
Heather Delfino

Pasteup
Adriana Longo

Printer
Worzalla Publishing Company
Stevens Point, Wisconsin

Illustrations
Halina Below-Spada: Back cover
John Mantha: p. 5

Photography acknowledgments
Cover: Jim Bryant
Mary Bredin: p.14(top); Jim Bryant: p.13(top and bottom), 22(top);
Ruth Malloy: p.20, 22(inset and bottom); Eric Melis: p.4;
Aymen Nader: p.6, 11(bottom right), 24, 25(bottom), 26(bottom), 29(top and bottom);
Courtesy of the Office of Tibet: p.26(top); Ron Watts/First Light: p.28(left);
Xu Jian: Title page, p.7, 8, 11(top left, right, and bottom left),12, 14(bottom), 15, 16, 17, 18, 19, 25(top), 27(left and right), 31.

For Alan Crabtree

951.5 / 1066

The Tibetan on the cover is a member of the world's last great nomadic society. The rare blue poppy on the title page grows only in the Himalayan Mountains. The motif that appears in the heading of every section reflects the unique style of Tibetan art. A *mandala* is shown on the back cover.

Cataloguing in Publication Data

Kalman, Bobbie, 1947-
   Tibet

(Lands, peoples, and cultures series)
Includes index.

ISBN 0-86505-213-1 (bound) ISBN 0-86505-293-X (pbk.)
1. Tibet (China) - Juvenile literature. 2. Tibet, Plateau of (China) - Description and travel - Juvenile literature.
I. Title. II. Series.

DS786.K35 1990   j951'.5

Published by
Crabtree Publishing Company

1110 Kamato Road	350 Fifth Avenue	73 Lime Walk
Unit 4	Suite 3308	Headington,
Mississauga, Ontario	New York	Oxford OX3 7AD
Canada L4W 2P3	N.Y. 10118	United Kingdom

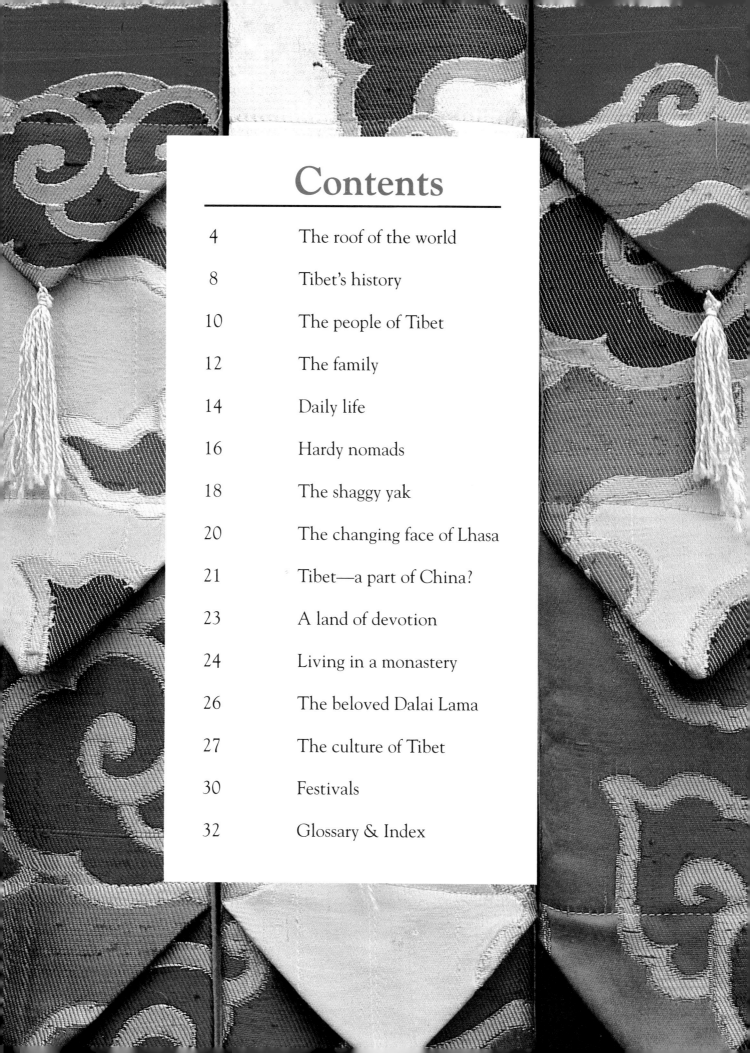

Contents

The roof of the world

Shrouded in mystery

No place on earth is quite like Tibet. For centuries this remote corner of the world was shrouded in mystery. Only a few adventurers attempted the long journey across difficult terrain and through dangerous mountain passes. Even now few outsiders are allowed to visit because Tibet is part of the People's Republic of China. The future of Tibet is also a mystery.

Tibet, known as "the roof of the world," is located in Central Asia on the world's highest and largest plateau. In summer the plateau is strewn with flower-filled pastures. In winter it seems a barren wasteland. Though harsh and forbidding, Tibet is also awe inspiring. Its vast grassy plains, towering mountain peaks, and crystal-clear lakes are unmatched in their natural beauty.

Living above the crowd

It is a wonder that anyone is able to live in this harsh environment. Yet, Tibetans have thrived here for more than two thousand years. On the plains, hardy nomads live in black tents made from yak hair; in the mountain valleys farming families till their terraced fields. People from all walks of life meet at local village markets to trade goods and exchange stories. Tibetans live difficult lives, but their religion and deep attachment to their homeland have given them the strength to survive.

Colorful prayer flags lead up to the Potala Palace, a massive, thirteen-story castle built on the side of the Red Hill overlooking the capital city of Lhasa. Its golden roof glows in the constant Tibetan sun. Inside, every wall is covered in hand-painted murals, and thousands of precious statues line the hallways. At one time the Potala Palace served as both government office and religious center, but now it is a museum.

A disappearing treasure

By far the most fascinating part of Tibet is its amazing culture. Tibet is the home of Lamaist Buddhism, a special form of the Buddhist religion whose priests are called lamas. The people of Tibet cherish their ancient religion. Unfortunately, since their country was taken over by China, most of the treasures that were part of Tibetan culture have been lost. Constant political turmoil threatens the very survival of the Tibetan people and their unique way of life.

The Plateau of Tibet

The entire Plateau of Tibet has a surface area of about 2 200 000 square kilometers (850,000 square miles), and its average height above sea level is a whopping 4000 meters (13,000 feet). Things look a lot different at such high altitudes. The sky is a deeper blue, and the clouds are much closer. The sunshine is intense, even though Tibet is not near the equator. At night the stars look extraordinarily bright.

Would you believe that the Plateau of Tibet was once at the bottom of a sea? About a hundred million years ago, that is exactly where it was. By the time the dinosaur age arrived, the sea had dried up, leaving behind many salty lakes. A tremendous shifting inside the earth forced up a huge area of land from underneath. This raised land became the Plateau of Tibet and the surrounding mountain ranges.

This map shows the Tibet Autonomous Region, which is now part of China. The country of Tibet was once much larger. When China took over, Tibet was divided up, so some areas are now part of Chinese provinces. The Plateau of Tibet extends well beyond the political borders indicated here.

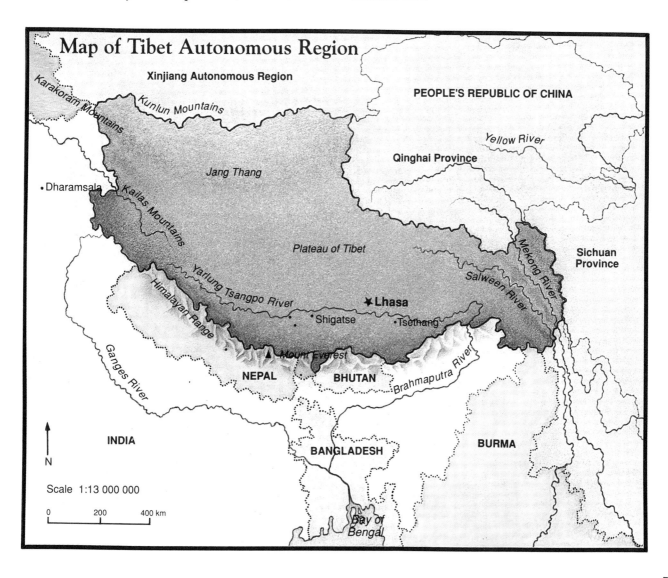

Map of Tibet Autonomous Region

- Xinjiang Autonomous Region
- Karakoram Mountains
- Kunlun Mountains
- PEOPLE'S REPUBLIC OF CHINA
- Yellow River
- Qinghai Province
- Jang Thang
- Dharamsala
- Kailas Mountains
- Plateau of Tibet
- Mekong River
- Sichuan Province
- Salween River
- Yarlung Tsangpo River
- Himalayan Range
- ★ Lhasa
- • Shigatse
- • Tsethang
- Ganges River
- ▲ Mount Everest
- NEPAL
- BHUTAN
- Brahmaputra River
- INDIA
- N
- BANGLADESH
- BURMA
- Scale 1:13 000 000
- 0   200   400 km
- Bay of Bengal

A rough and tough terrain

The Plateau of Tibet can be divided into three separate areas. The large northern part of the plateau, called the Jang Thang (pronounced Chang Tang), extends into the Chinese province of Qinghai. Cold winds blow constantly across this plain. Most of the rough ground consists of a vast grassland, and frozen desert covers the rest. There are no rivers, but salty lakes and marshes dot the landscape. For the most part the chilly Jang Thang is uninhabited. Small groups of nomads roam the southern and eastern grasslands, which are ideal for grazing animals such as yaks and sheep. South and east of the Jang Thang is the Outer Plateau, where most Tibetans now live. This region is known as the heartland of Tibet because good crops thrive in the farmers' fields of the many river valleys.

Gorgeous gorges

The foothills and gorges make up the third and smallest region of the plateau. Water, which comes tumbling out of Tibet's mountains, wears deep grooves into the land. These grooves eventually become gorges, or deep valleys bordered by cliffs. Rivers run through these rocky gorges. This area is lower than the rest of Tibet, but even at its lowest point it is still 1615 meters (5,300 feet) above sea level. Unlike the Jang Thang, thick forests and lush vegetation cover most of this region.

Rimmed by ranges

Tibet is rimmed by mountain ranges on three sides. These mountains serve as natural borders. Along the south the Himalayan range, which stretches 2415 kilometers (1,500 miles), separates Tibet from India, Nepal, Burma, and Bhutan. Mount Everest, the highest peak in the world, is located on the border between Tibet and Nepal. Its summit is 8848 meters (29,029 feet) high. The Karakoram Mountains extend along the western side of Tibet, north of the Himalayas. Beyond the Kunlun Mountains in the north is the Xinjiang Autonomous Region.

Although harsh and forbidding, the Plateau of Tibet has a beauty all its own. Most areas are flat, but some areas have rolling hills and glacial lakes.

Asia's main water source

Several of Asia's major river systems begin on the Plateau of Tibet or among the surrounding mountains. The Yarlung Tsangpo River cuts across Tibet and then makes a sharp turn south. At this point it becomes the Brahmaputra River, which flows through India and Bangladesh. The sources of India's other great rivers, the Indus and the Ganges, are also found in the Kailas Mountains in western Tibet. The Yangtze River forms the eastern border of present-day Tibet and winds its way through the heartland of China. China's great Yellow River begins on the plateau as well. The remaining main rivers, the Salween and Mekong, are found in eastern Tibet.

Lots of sun and wind

Because of its high altitude, Tibet is a cold place. Constant chilly winds sweep across the rolling hills and plains of the plateau. Blizzards and hailstorms are common. Up in the mountains it is always bitterly cold (-40°C, -40°F), but the valleys can be quite pleasant because of their sheltered, southern locations. Lhasa, the capital city, is located in a valley, so it enjoys average midsummer temperatures of around 17°C (63°F). In some areas the temperature can change both rapidly and often during any given day because of the winds. Within minutes it can fall from 29°C to 4°C (84°F to 39°F).

Tibet receives little precipitation. It rarely snows in the mountains, and only light rainfall reaches the plateau in the summer. Most of the rain falls in the forested region of the foothills and gorges.

Agriculture

According to a legend the very first Tibetan planted a field near the present-day town of Tsethang. Some farmers visit this site every year before planting season begins. For good luck they take a handful of earth from the "first field" and sprinkle it over their own fields.

Because Tibet receives an extraordinary amount of sunlight, crops are giant-sized. Imagine digging up a potato that weighs two kilograms (almost five pounds)!

Much of the plateau is desert, and even the conditions in the fertile valleys are far from ideal. The high altitudes shorten the growing season to less than one hundred frost-free days a year. There is plenty of sun, however. Tibet receives about eight hours of sun every day. As a result, giant-sized vegetables are harvested.

Only the hardiest crops can be grown in Tibet's unique conditions. Barley is the most important crop of all. Millet, rapeseed, and corn are also planted. Sturdy types of fruits and vegetables such as tomatoes, potatoes, and cabbage have recently been introduced with success. The foothills of eastern Tibet enjoy almost tropical conditions, so crops such as rice and bananas are common there. This area also produces cash crops such as peanuts, tea, and tobacco, which are sold in other parts of the world.

 # Tibet's history

No one knows for certain when people began living in Tibet because Tibet's recorded history only dates back as far as the seventh century. At that time Tibet was twice the size it is today and was made up of many small kingdoms. These kingdoms were ruled by kings who often fought battles against one another for land and power. Tribes of nomads lived on the grasslands of the plateau, following their herds whenever there was a change of season.

Songtsen Gampo unifies Tibet

The most famous figure of early Tibetan history is a warrior king named Songtsen Gampo. He united all the Tibetan tribes. He built a fortress on the Red Hill overlooking the ancient city of Lhasa. He also made up laws and established the Tibetan writing system.

(above) For centuries monks held powerful positions in Tibet. Today their political power has been taken away.

During Songtsen Gampo's reign Tibet gained control over Nepal and parts of China. To strengthen his ties with these nearby countries, the king married two princesses. Princess Brikuti Devi came from Nepal, and Wen Cheng was the daughter of the emperor of China. They each brought a precious statue of Buddha to Tibet. Together the princesses converted the king to Buddhism. Under their influence Buddhism spread throughout Tibet.

Lamaist Buddhism

Over the centuries Tibetan Buddhism came to be known as Lamaist Buddhism. Throughout the country Tibetans built monasteries high up on the mountainsides. Special monks called lamas ran the monasteries. The monks and nuns who lived there led religious lives, performed ceremonies, and acted as spiritual guides to the Tibetan people.

The time of the Mongols

Tibet was often invaded by fierce Mongol warriors. In 1280 the Mongols invaded China and Tibet and established the Yuan dynasty. The famous Mongol emperor Kublai Khan greatly admired the high lamas of Tibet and encouraged his subjects to adopt Lamaist Buddhism. In the fourteenth century a Tibetan religious leader named Tsong Khapa formed an order of monks known as the Yellow Hats. With the help of the Mongols, these monks soon became very powerful.

Wise rulers

In 1578 a great teacher of the Yellow Hats, Sonam Gyatso, received the honorary title "Dalai" from Altan Khan, the great-great grandson of Kublai Khan. *Dalai* means "ocean of wisdom." The title "Dalai Lama" was passed on to his successors. The fifth Dalai Lama became the first Dalai Lama to rule Tibet as a religious king. He had the magnificent Potala Palace built, which became his residence and served as the main government building. (See picture on page 4.) The Great Fifth also set up a system of government that lasted until the middle of this century. His court consisted of lamas, nobles, and governors who were in charge of collecting taxes. From time to time Chinese dynasties had influence in Tibet.

A new order

At the beginning of the twentieth century the thirteenth Dalai Lama became very concerned about the state of his country. He tried to modernize Tibet by firing corrupt officials, lifting harsh punishments, building roads, and opening schools. For forty years, while China was involved with its own struggles, Tibet was left alone. In 1949, however, China became a communist country, and the government was eager to make Tibet part of new China. Chinese troops soon entered Lhasa.

When China took over, it promised to respect the Tibetan people and the position of the Dalai Lama. Yet the new government introduced changes that threatened the traditional Tibetan way of life. The Tibetans resisted, and a rebellion broke out in 1959. Fearing for his life, the young fourteenth Dalai Lama fled to Dharamsala, India. Chinese forces defeated the Tibetans and closed the borders to outsiders.

Big changes, good and bad

The Chinese, along with Tibetan work crews, started work on grand projects. Roads were built, military bases were established, and farming and herding communes were created. Schools, factories, and hospitals were opened in large villages. Unfortunately, a vast amount of destruction also occurred. The new government frowned on religion, so most of the monasteries and temples were torn down. Thousands of people were thrown in jail and left there for years. Others were tortured and killed.

Tibet Autonomous Region

Today the Chinese government considers Tibet to be an autonomous region within China. Autonomous means independent, but Tibetans are not happy with the amount of independence they have. China controls all government policies, laws, education, and the media. It is unlikely that China would ever grant Tibet the freedom to exist as an independent nation. Tibet is too valuable as a source of natural resources and as a military base for defending borders.

Lack of freedom

In the fall of 1987 the Tibetans staged an uprising against the government in the streets of Lhasa. Many people were killed. Other demonstrations followed, the biggest of which was held in March 1989. Since then Tibet has been under martial law, which means that Chinese soldiers rule Tibet. Its borders are closed, and no one can travel around Tibet without a special permit.

The Chinese government treats the Chinese people in a similar way. In June 1989 Chinese students rallied in the capital city of Beijing to protest their lack of freedom. The Chinese army crushed this huge but peaceful demonstration with tanks and guns. Tibetans and Chinese alike share a hope for more freedom.

The people of Tibet

About six million Tibetans live in greater Tibet, two million of whom live in the Tibet Autonomous Region. The majority of Tibetans are farmers who live in ancient villages scattered along the river valleys. Other Tibetans make the capital city of Lhasa their home. The rest of the population consists of nomadic tribes.

Although Tibetans are distant relatives of the Mongols and Burmese, they have distinctive looks. Their high cheekbones, black hair, and sturdy build set them apart. Besides a common ancestry, Tibetans also share the same language, religion, and culture. During many centuries of isolation from the rest of the world, Tibetans have developed their own national character.

A proud people

For ages nomads ruled the grasslands of Tibet. At one time these people were fierce warriors who invaded distant territories. After being introduced to the Buddhist religion, they became peace-loving people. The challenging nomadic life still requires courage, but the gentle spirit of the Tibetan nomads is reflected in their easy-going and friendly personalities. One large soldier-like tribe called the Khampa lives in eastern Tibet. Nomads, especially the Khampa, are known for their horsemanship. Their horses wear intricately embroidered riding gear made by the men in their spare time. Many nomads make long pilgrimages, or religious journeys, to temples and monasteries.

A harsh homeland

The harsh Tibetan climate is reflected in the faces of the people who live there. The sun and wind have lined and cracked their skin. To protect themselves from the sun's harsh rays, Tibetans often smear yak butter on their faces. They also wear scarves or masks to keep out the dust. Their clothes are well suited to the changeable climate. Tibetans bundle up against the cold with sheepskin coats and knee-high boots made from yak hide. People wear several layers of clothing so they can easily take off or add a layer or two when the weather changes during the day.

Adapting to special conditions

Visitors to Tibet often suffer from "mountain sickness." Mountain sickness makes you feel dizzy and sick to your stomach. It is caused by the lack of oxygen in the air. In order to survive, all living things need oxygen. When you breathe, your lungs absorb oxygen from the air. At sea level there is plenty of oxygen, but as air rises it contains less and less of this gas. In Tibet the amount of oxygen in the air is very low because the plateau is high above sea level. Although visitors suffer from mountain sickness, Tibetans never do. After living in Tibet for so long, their bodies have adapted to the special conditions. Their blood contains extra red blood cells, which allow their lungs to absorb more oxygen in one breath than the lungs of people who live at lower altitudes can. Scientists think that the Tibetans have adapted to the high altitudes in other ways as well, but these have not yet been discovered.

The Chinese presence

In the last thirty years many Chinese people have moved to Tibet. Most have been sent there by the government to develop and govern this new region of China. The Chinese residents run factories, schools, and hotels. They work as tour guides, engineers, and government officials. A small number have made Tibet their permanent home. Most of the Chinese, however, only stay for work terms of up to three years, and these workers are then replaced by others. In addition, about 300,000 Chinese soldiers are stationed at army bases throughout the region. Both soldiers and Chinese people on work terms are not counted in the official population. As a result, the Chinese outnumber the Tibetans in many places, but the recorded population figures do not show this.

The young boy (below) wears blue clothing supplied by the Chinese. His friend wears the traditional Tibetan chupa. The woman (bottom) sports a braided head band with coral and turquoise stones.

The horseman (above) is a member of the brave Khampa tribe of eastern Tibet. The harsh life on the Plateau of Tibet (top) is reflected in the deep lines on the face of an old woman.

 # The family

The Tibetan home is crowded with people. Whether in yak-hair tents or city apartments, several generations of families usually live together. Children share their homes with their parents, grandparents, and sometimes a few uncles and aunts. The extended family is common in Tibet because the bonds between family members are strong. A young couple rarely sets up a new home or, as Tibetans say, "starts a new kitchen." Instead, a woman moves in with her husband's family, or else he comes to live with hers. Either way, Tibetan homes are busy places full of loving people.

Getting married

Once a young man reaches the age of eighteen, his family starts searching for a marriage partner for him. When someone suitable has been found, the two families visit each other several times, always bearing gifts such as butter, cheese, or meat. A monk checks the couple's horoscopes to ensure that the partners will make a good match. He also picks the best date and time for the wedding. Once all this is done, the marriage papers can be signed. Although the parents arrange the marriage, it does not take place if the man or woman protests.

Will she or won't she?

A traditional Tibetan wedding involves much play-acting. On the appointed day the groom's family travels to the bride's home. The bride's family pretends to be surprised and tells the visitors to leave. The visitors say they will not go without the bride, and a big argument builds up. Sometimes the wailing bride gets caught in a tug-of-war—her mother pulling on one arm and the groom pulling on the other!

Leaving home

The bride finally leaves her home on a horse or a white yak. She and the groom are accompanied by his family. Everyone hopes that no snow or rain will fall before the ceremony because precipitation is thought to bring bad luck. When she arrives at the groom's family home, the bride pretends to be very upset. Sometimes she really is upset because she misses her parents. She cries and weeps—nothing can make her feel better. Finally she calms down and accepts a pail of milk from her mother-in-law. She flicks a few drops of milk into the air for good luck. The ceremony can now be conducted with chants, prayers, food, and offerings. Everyone is in a good mood, so the feasting begins. The eating, drinking, and dancing sometimes last for ten days.

Including children

Children are considered to be important members of the family group. They are included in work and play, parties and picnics. Tibetans do not have many children, so they are very pleased when a son or daughter is born. A few days after the birth, friends and neighbors visit the family's house to bring clothes for the newborn and a religious offering for the mother.

About a month after the birth, a lucky day is chosen for the baby to go outside. To ward off evil, a dab of soot is rubbed onto the baby's nose. The baby is then named in a ceremony conducted by a monk. Children often receive meaningful names such as Tsering, which means "long life," Dikyi meaning "happiness," or Trashi meaning "good luck."

Sticking together

Life can be difficult in Tibet because the weather is harsh, and most Tibetans are poor. Family members stick together and help one another. When children grow up, they support their aging parents. In turn, grandparents look after their grandchildren while the parents work. Tibetans love children and look forward to the day when they can devote all their time to caring for the little ones.

(opposite) In the valleys of southeastern Tibet, families such as this one live in wooden houses that stand on stilts.

(above) Grandparents often babysit while parents work.

(right) Because of the harsh Tibetan wind, this child's skin has already begun to acquire wrinkles.

Daily life

Traditional Tibetan homes

Most Tibetans live in earthen homes because other building materials are not available. Traditional houses have two stories and flat roofs. They are often built against the sides of mountains, so they almost look as if they are part of the natural landscape. The whole house is whitewashed except for the window frames. Window frames and wooden pillars and joints are painted in exquisite designs of bright red, blue, and yellow. Many people also place flower boxes outside their windows. Some windows have glass panes, but most are covered with cloth or waxed paper and protected by wooden shutters.

(left) Every day this woman spins wool for making clothes.

(below) Other daily chores include doing the laundry by hand, cooking, cleaning, and tending animals.

Spacious interiors

Tibetan homes are spacious inside. The kitchen and storeroom on the main floor contain a few storage cupboards, a finely crafted cabinet, and a low table. These main pieces of furniture are decorated with ornate carvings and inlay work. On the sunny second floor are the living quarters. To keep warm, everyone sleeps together in one big room.

The comforts of home

The living conditions of most Tibetans are simple. Their homes are equipped with very few modern conveniences. The houses are heated by fires, but chimneys are rare. The smoke drifts through the house and out the door and windows. Dried yak dung is used as fuel because wood is hard to find on the barren plateau. Most Tibetans go to bed when the sun sets because they have no electric light. Only recently constructed homes have electricity and running water. People carry their daily supply of water from a pump, well, or nearby stream. They use outdoor toilets.

The sacred altar

Every Tibetan home has a sacred altar. Family members go to this quiet corner to worship and make offerings each day. Bowls of water and food are placed in front of Buddhist statues along with incense burners and yak-butter lamps. Religious paintings hang on the walls.

Basic fare

Although their diet lacks variety, Tibetans have a hearty appetite for their favorite foods. Tibetans young and old relish yak-butter tea. A single person may drink as many as forty cups of this frothy broth in one day. After boiling the tea with water and soda, the tea maker mixes it with yak butter and salt in a tall churn.

Most Tibetans eat with chopsticks or spoons. Roasted barley flour, called *tsampa*, is the staple at almost every meal. A small amount of *tsampa* is poured into a wooden bowl and mixed with tea, yak butter, or cheese. The mixture is kneaded into little balls and then eaten by hand. A piece of yak meat or mutton may be served along with it.

Going to school

The Tibetan language existed long before it was ever written down. The Tibetan alphabet, developed in the seventh century, was based on the Indian Sanscrit alphabet. Nearly three quarters of Tibetans are unable to read or write. Schools are open for all to attend, but many farming and nomad families live too far away. Tibetan is only taught as a second language. Chinese is the language used in high school and university, making it hard for Tibetans to go on to higher education.

(above) Although young and old may not always dress alike, they often work together side by side.

15

Hardy nomads

Imagine camping out every night of your life. Tibetan nomads do! The life of a nomad is not a vacation, however. It is a challenging existence. The nomads of Tibet live in remote areas of the Tibetan Plateau, following their herds from pasture to pasture. About one third of Tibet is inhabited by scattered groups of these hardy people. Approximately half a million nomads live in Tibet today. They are the world's last great nomadic society.

Tibetan nomads are not always on the move. They stay in one location during winter, spring, and summer. In fall they herd their animals from pasture to pasture through a vast territory. When it is time to move on, the nomads pack up every last belonging and form a large caravan. Reaching their new pasture, they set up camp again. It takes about half a day to erect a single tent.

A tent called home

Yak-hair tents are ideal shelters on the lofty, windswept plains because they keep out the wind. These huge, black dwellings are woven from the short inner hair of yaks. The tent is not meant just for sleeping; it is the center of daily life. This movable home is furnished with a finely crafted wooden chest, a low table, and storage boxes. The family sets up an altar where butter lamps burn all day long. Pots and pans, utensils, a butter churn, a weaving loom, and a small stove are all part of the furnishings. A vent at the top of the tent allows smoke from the stove to escape. Some nomads build storage sheds and permanent houses in their home areas.

(above) These nomads pose for a picture during a picnic festival. The white tent is only put up for special occasions such as this. Tents for everyday use are black.

Setting up camp

Several families often live in one camp. The tents are built in a circle, with a firepit in the center. The men usually sleep outside by the fire, and the women and children sleep in the tents. In winter a wall made of yak dung or stone is built around the tents to keep out the wind. An animal compound is set up some distance from the tents. Besides yaks, nomads keep other types of livestock. Goats and sheep add variety to the Tibetan diet. Sheep also provide wool for blankets and clothes. Many nomads own horses, as well.

Daily life

The women of the camp get up early to milk the yaks, goats, and sheep. The men light the fire. To begin the day some barley flour or juniper branches are burned as an offering to the spirits. The whole camp eats breakfast together. The men then go out to pasture with the herd, and the women and children stay at the camp. The women spend a great deal of time sewing, mending, spinning, and weaving. In the evening the main meal brings everyone together again. It is a relaxing time, enlivened by stories and music, jokes and laughter.

Trading trips

From time to time the nomad group ventures to town to trade with the local farmers. The nomads exchange their meat products for barley and tea. Some sell medicinal herbs that they have gathered; others trade salt collected from the salt lakes on the plateau. For years the Tibetan nomads have supplied their country-folk with all the salt they need. It takes them about a month to gather and transport it to local markets. Sometimes they sell the salt to markets in Nepal, Bhutan, and India.

(above) Nomads call themselves **drogpa.** *This young* **drogpa,** *dressed in the traditional* **chupa,** *sets down the load he has been carrying. In fall the* **drogpa** *move their camp from place to place with their animals or take long pilgrimages to Lhasa and other holy places.*

The shaggy yak

In the highlands of central Asia lives a most extraordinary animal—the yak. The yak is a shaggy beast that is perfectly at home way up in the Himalayan mountains as well as on the Tibetan Plateau. You might find it difficult living at such a high altitude, but the yak would be unhappy anywhere else.

Yaks have a special kind of blood that helps them cope with the thin mountain air. They can absorb more oxygen than we can because they have more red blood cells. Yaks are also well suited to the cold mountain climate because they have plenty of hair to keep them warm. Their reddish-black hair is so long that these animals look as if they are wearing big fur coats. When a yak lies down on the ground, its fur acts as a protective mat.

Wild days are gone

At one time huge herds of wild yaks roamed freely from one end of the Tibetan Plateau to the other. There were as many as two hundred thousand, but now only about twenty thousand are left. Most were killed by Chinese soldiers. Wild yaks look mighty because they stand almost two meters (six feet) tall and weigh about five hundred kilograms (1,100 pounds). They also have curved horns that grow to a hundred centimeters (forty inches) long. Some wild yaks live to be twenty-five years old. Today wild yaks are a rare sight; they can only be seen way up in the remote mountains.

A female yak, called a **dri**, *is milked three times a day. When a* **dri** *has a baby yak, the nomads only milk three teets so one is left for the baby yak.*

18

Beasts of burden

Over the centuries the Tibetans have bred yaks for their own purposes. About two million of these domesticated yaks, which are smaller than their wild cousins, live on the plateau. Tamed yaks are used in countless ways, and the Tibetans value them above any other animal. Surefooted and strong, yaks make excellent pack animals. They can carry extremely heavy loads across treacherous mountain passes. Instead of riding their yaks, Tibetans walk alongside their animals.

The indispensable yak

The yak is more than just a helpful beast of burden. It also provides Tibetans with everything from food to fuel. Although yak milk is rarely drunk as a beverage, it is turned into all sorts of nutritious dairy products, such as yogurt, cheese, and butter. Yak butter is an essential ingredient in Tibetan-style tea. The pale glow of yak-butter candles is a constant presence in temples and on family altars. To meet the daily dairy needs of Tibetans, yaks are milked three times a day.

Yaks also provide Tibetans with clothes and blankets. Tibetans spin the fine underhair into wool, which is then woven into cloth. The long outer hair is used for making ropes. Unlike sheep, yaks are not shorn. Instead, the nomads simply cut the hair, always careful to leave some behind to protect the animals from the cold. Tibetans make felt by pounding dampened yak hair into thick, coarse sheets. When a yak dies, its hide is used to make all sorts of leather goods, such as boots, belts, laces, saddles, and saddlebags. Yak butter is used to tan, or soften, the hide. Special square boats are made from yak hide by sewing several hides together and stretching them over square wooden frames. These boats are used to ferry people across the smooth glacial lakes.

Not a single yak or yak product goes to waste. Yak meat is dried or smoked so it can be stored for a long time without going bad. Even yak dung is collected, dried, and burned as fuel.

Name that yak!

The yak belongs to the family of *bos grunniens*, which means "grunting ox," because that is the sound it makes. Wild yaks are known as *bos grunniens mutus*. Perhaps they have a longer name because they are bigger! The word "yak" comes from the Tibetan word *gyag*, which refers only to pure-blooded male yaks. Female yaks are called *dri* in Tibet and *nak* in Nepal, and yak bulls are called *boa*. And just to add to the confusion, the whole yak family is called *nor*, which means "wealth." And that is still not the end of all this yakkety-yak. If a yak has been cross-bred with an ox, it is called a *dzo*. *Dzo*, do you have the *nak* to learn all these "yak-facts?" We do not want to *gyag* you with so many details. *Nor* do we want to grunt on any more about these bashful *bos*! Don't you a*dri*?

The changing face of Lhasa

Since the sixth century Lhasa has been the Tibetan center for trade, government, and religious activity. Located along the Kyichu River at 3660 meters (12,000 feet) above sea level, this city became the core of the kingdom. The magnificent Potala Palace adorns the city like a crown. For centuries traders, nomads, and pilgrims have come from far and wide to trade their wares or visit the holy sites. Today many people come and go, making Lhasa a very crowded and active place.

For centuries the exact location of Lhasa was unknown. Recent changes have drastically altered the face of mysterious Lhasa. With a small population of 200,000 people, only 50,000 of which are Tibetan, Lhasa is the only Tibetan center big enough to be called a city. Tibetans and a small Muslim community live in the older section of the city. A new section houses the growing Chinese population.

Busy markets and narrow lanes

The Barkhor Bazaar is the main street in the old section of the city. Lined with numerous small shops, the street makes a full circle around the Jokhang Temple. Street vendors display their wares on tables or on blankets on the ground. Canopies shelter the traders from the strong sun. Merchants sell everything from yak cheese to handmade carpets.

This noisy, crowded street is full of all sorts of interesting people. Pilgrims twirling prayer wheels make their way around the temple in a clockwise direction. Groups of nomads can be seen sitting in circles taking meals together. In the evening monks gather to chant and pray.

Down the narrow lanes old buildings lean away from the cobblestone streets, and flower boxes sit on intricately painted windowsills.

New Lhasa

In recent years Lhasa has expanded, forming a new city. Broad, tree-lined streets lead into recently created neighborhoods. Signs of modern city living such as hydro-poles, traffic lights, pavement, and concrete are becoming common. Low-rise, brick apartments have been built to house the Chinese residents. Many other buildings such as government offices, banks, schools, and hospitals have appeared on the scene. Lhasa also boasts a radio and television station, a satellite dish, and a nearby airport.

Increased industry

The Chinese population and a small number of Tibetans are involved with types of industry that have never been seen before in Tibet. When the Chinese first arrived, thousands of Tibetans helped construct new roads and buildings. As Lhasa continues to grow, large construction crews are still busy. Small factories have been set up in and around Lhasa. These workshops produce shoes, carpets, matches, batteries, glass, and cement. Many people also run shops, restaurants, and inns.

All roads lead to Lhasa

The construction of a road system transformed Tibet's transportation. Today roads crisscross Tibet, and narrow highways wind their way through steep mountain passes. Almost all the roads lead to Lhasa. Carts and bicycles are popular on the streets of Lhasa and other towns. Only government officials and foreigners can afford cars and jeeps.

Tibet—a part of China?

For over thirty years the unwelcome Chinese government has controlled the lives of Tibetans. Tibetans want to rule their own country, but China does not want to leave, and Tibet is not strong enough to force out her mighty neighbor. Tibetans would not be so angry if China had been fair to them, but many people have suffered under Chinese rule.

It is estimated that over one million Tibetans lost their lives in the early years of Chinese rule. Others were imprisoned or forced to work in gangs. Anyone who spoke against the Chinese government was severely punished. Widespread crop failure occurred because Tibetan farmers were ordered to grow wheat and rice instead of hardy barley. Tibetans starved while their harvests were shipped out to feed highly populated China.

The end of a unique culture?

Perhaps saddest of all was that Tibetans were denied their culture. They were forbidden to practice their religion and forced to speak Chinese. Many masterpieces of Tibetan art were destroyed. About ninety percent of the ancient monasteries were burned to the ground or reduced to rubble, precious statues were smashed, and temples were used for grain storage. The new government did everything in its power to eliminate traditional Tibetan ways and replace them with Chinese ways. Within a short time the Tibetan culture was almost completely lost.

Improvements for some

After 1980 life in Tibet began to improve. Some prisoners were released, lands and animals were returned to their owners, and religion was permitted. Some businesses began to prosper. Electricity and manufactured goods became available. Transportation, health care, and education improved. Despite all this aid the economy in Tibet is still in bad shape. The money that has been spent on developing Tibet has hardly helped the Tibetans at all. The Chinese residents get the good jobs, whereas many Tibetans still live in poverty. Rarely do Tibetans receive the kinds of homes or special privileges that the Chinese do.

Benefits out of balance

China benefits from Tibet in many ways. Much of Tibet's art and precious antiques were either destroyed or sold overseas. The huge profits were kept by the Chinese government. Tibet's natural resources such as coal, iron, peat, and salt, and its huge forested areas are worth billions of dollars to China. The Tibetan Plateau is also valuable to China as a space for testing nuclear weapons and dumping nuclear wastes. The resulting radioactivity is damaging the environment and endangering the health of the people and animals that live in Tibet.

Living in an occupied land

The strained relationship between the Chinese and Tibetans can make day-to-day life in Tibet both difficult and dangerous. Chinese soldiers are everywhere. No one feels safe or secure. The Chinese residents believe that Tibet is part of their rightful homeland, but the Tibetans want them to leave. As a result, Tibetan and Chinese neighbors are often angry with one another.

The world is watching

Nothing can justify the unfair and often brutal treatment Tibetans receive. Treated as second-class citizens in their own land, Tibetans have been denied self-government, freedom of speech, and freedom of religion. Any Tibetan who openly practices religion is denied good job opportunities. Tibetans are not permitted to teach Lamaist Buddhism to their children. People are imprisoned and even executed without fair trials. Concerned people around the world are trying to help by pressuring the Chinese government into dealing fairly with the people who have lived on the roof of the world for thousands of years.

(center) In Tibet, stones with prayers written on them are used to ward off evil spirits. This practice comes from ancient Tibetan folk beliefs.

The Pango Chorten located in Gyantse is one of the largest in Tibet. Chortens contain relics of lamas or other holy items.

(below) Every day the courtyard in front of the Jokhang Temple is filled with worshippers who lie face down to show their devotion.

A land of devotion

Tibetans are deeply religious. Monks, farmers, and nomads alike practice Buddhism, a religion that has transformed life in Tibet. As the Tibetans themselves say, Buddhism changed them from a warlike people to a peace-loving, friendly people.

Ancient Tibetan beliefs

Long before Buddhism came to their land, the Tibetans believed in a folk religion called Bon. Every day they faced the powerful forces of nature in their harsh homeland. In early times the people believed that gods or spirits dwelt in these forces and in every mountain, wind, stream, tree, and rock. Many rituals, such as offerings and sacrifices, were performed to influence and appease the spirits of nature.

Buddhist beliefs

Buddhism reached Tibet in the seventh century. This ancient religion was founded in India by a wandering religious man known as Buddha. *Buddha* means "The Awakened One." Buddhists believe in reincarnation, which is the cycle of birth, death, and rebirth. When a person dies, he or she is believed to be reborn as another person, animal, or insect. The aim of all Buddhists is to end this cycle and achieve *nirvana*, a state of supreme happiness. The Buddha taught that people could reach *nirvana* through prayer, meditation, and good behavior, and by helping others and seeking wisdom.

Lamaist Buddhism

The Tibetan religion is sometimes known as Lamaist Buddhism because its leaders are called lamas. The Tibetans do not just follow the teachings of Buddha. They also believe in the many spirits and magical powers that were once part of the Bon religion. For example, at one time piles of stones were left at mountain passes for the mountain spirits to ensure safe journeys. Today Lamaist Buddhists leave *mani* stones with *mantras* written on them. A *mantra* is a short prayer that is repeated over and over.

Lamaist Buddhists also believe in two other kinds of supernatural beings: spiritual protectors and *bodhisattvas*. *Bodhisattvas* are wise and kind, so Tibetans pray to them for guidance. Many devout worshippers lie face down on the ground in front of statues of *bodhisattvas* to honor these compassionate beings. The statues of *bodhisattvas* look kind, but statues of the protectors can look angry and fierce. No Tibetan would be frightened, though. The more fierce a protector looks, the more likely he is to frighten away evil.

Religious objects

All over Tibet colorful prayer flags are tied to trees, rooftops, and poles. Prayer flags have Buddhist scriptures written on them. Tibetans also carry around prayer wheels. Inside the wheel is a *mantra* written on a piece of paper. The owner twirls the wheel around and around as often as possible. Tibetans believe that every time a prayer wheel turns, or a prayer flag flutters in the wind, a prayer is sent up to the heavens. Prayer wheels are also found in streams and in rows along temple walls.

Holy temples

A Tibetan temple is guarded by statues of several spiritual protectors. The temple itself is filled with the distinctive odor of yak butter and incense. It is quite dark inside because yak-butter lamps provide the only lighting. Huge murals cover the walls, and golden statues line the passageways. The altar contains large statues of the Buddha. Worshippers walk around the statues in a clockwise direction and drape *khata* over them. *Khata* are white scarves that are offered as signs of peace. Many worshippers chant the *mantra* "Om mani padme hum," which means "Hail to the jewel in the lotus." Some people go to the temples every day to fill up the lamps with offerings of yak butter. Pilgrims travel great distances to visit the most important temples, such as the Jokhang Temple in Lhasa.

 # Living in a monastery

Long before dawn the deep sound of a conch-shell horn drifts through the sleeping monastery. Tsering, a young monk, rubs his eyes and scrambles out of bed. There is no heat or electricity, so he shivers for a moment in the early-morning air. He quickly puts on his heavy robes in the dark. Leaving his cell, Tsering joins the other monks. Each monk wears a maroon robe and has short-cropped hair, just as Tsering does.

The day always begins in the prayer hall. Yak-butter lamps glow in the dark room as several dozen monks chant *mantras*. Cymbals and drums accompany the sound of their chanting voices. Sometimes the sessions last for three hours! During the prayer session Tsering passes out a bit of breakfast to the older monks. It consists of yak-butter tea and some *tsampa*.

A monk's life

The life of a monk or nun has never been easy. Rising before dawn, the monks and nuns of the past were kept busy with religious activities and the chores of community life. Some monks spent long hours in study and prayer; others worked as artists, clerks, artisans, builders, cooks, teachers, and housekeepers. Besides doing their work, they meditated, studied the scriptures, and chanted *mantras*.

Anyone was welcome to join a monastery. Boys joined when they were seven and girls when they were ten. Each family tried to send at least one child. Sending a son or daughter brought honor to the family and enabled the child to receive a religious education.

Tsering spends part of every day studying the sacred Buddhist scriptures from handmade Tibetan books.

The cultural core of Tibet

At one time Tibet was filled with monasteries. Some were huge estates with thousands of monks in each. People who wanted to lead a religious way of life became monks or nuns and lived together in these communities. Monasteries also developed and preserved the Tibetan culture. The greatest Tibetan poets, artists, sculptors, and musicians were monks. Monks served several functions in traditional Tibetan society. Their main duties consisted of performing religious rituals and providing spiritual guidance to the large Buddhist population. Some monks assisted in ruling the country, but this is no longer the case.

Tsering's dream

In recent years the lives of monks have changed drastically. Tsering feels lucky to have been able to join a monastery at all. After China took over Tibet in 1951, all the monasteries were closed up. Most of the buildings were destroyed, and now only a few people are allowed to become monks or nuns. To support the monastery, Tsering spends most of his day working in the orchard. This means he has very little time for religious studies. Tsering hopes that someday the Dalai Lama will return to Tibet, and the monasteries will once again be filled with monks and nuns.

(above) The most respected monks are honored with the title "lama." All lamas are monks, but not all monks are lamas.

(below) These students are trying to win scholarly arguments. The art of debate is part of every monk's training. After making a good point, a monk claps three times.

The beloved Dalai Lama

Despite the hardships the Tibetan people are forced to undergo, they still hope for a bright future. The leader in whom they place their hope is the fourteenth Dalai Lama. For centuries the Dalai Lama was the ruler and spiritual leader of Tibet. Today His Holiness the Dalai Lama is still the spiritual leader of Tibet. His real name is Tenzin Gyatso.

(bottom) In Tibetan temples, photographs of the Dalai Lama are often placed on the altar.

(below) His Holiness the Dalai Lama lives in India but devotes his time to helping Tibetans and promoting peace.

The Tibetan people are devoted to their beloved leader. They have not seen him for many years, however, because he fled to India after China took over. Tibetans treasure pictures of the Dalai Lama as a sign of hope. They place his picture on their home altars or carry one in their pockets. Some children wear pictures of the Dalai Lama around their necks.

How to find a Dalai Lama

The Dalai Lama is believed to be the reincarnation of Chenrezig, the *bodhisattva* of compassion. When a Dalai Lama dies, Tibetans believe that he is reborn as a young child somewhere in Tibet. Finding the new Dalai Lama can be a difficult task. Nobody knows who the next one will be. High lamas are assigned the job of finding him. Wearing disguises, they look for a boy with big ears, long eyes, and a special birthmark. When they find such a child, he is asked to identify the previous Dalai Lama's possessions from a collection of objects. Once the high lamas feel sure that they have found the real Dalai Lama, they bring him to the Potala Palace in Lhasa to be educated as the new ruler and spiritual leader of Tibet.

A man of peace

His Holiness the Dalai Lama works hard telling the world about the plight of the Tibetan people. He believes that Tibetans must win over their enemies through kindness instead of fighting and violence. In 1989 he was awarded the Nobel Peace Prize for the peaceful ways in which he attempts to bring about freedom for his people. The prize was also given in recognition of his respect for all living things. Although the Dalai Lama is a very important person, he is friendly and loves children. He would enjoy receiving a letter from you. You can write to him at the following address:
The Office of His Holiness the Dalai Lama, Thekchen Choling, P.O. McCleod, Dharamsala (H. P.), INDIA.

The culture of Tibet

In Tibet and India, Tibetans are trying to preserve ancient traditions and recreate artwork in the Tibetan style. When permitted, monks and ordinary Tibetans work hard to restore the buildings and paintings that remain. Nearly all Tibetan works of art are of a religious nature. The walls of the temples and monasteries that survive are covered in painted murals and banners. Beams are decorated with intricate designs, and rows of golden statues adorn the passageways. The humble monks who produced these great works did not sign their names on their creations. It was enough to create masterpieces that inspired all who saw them.

Traditional shows

Tibetans love to attend and perform in colorful and exciting shows. The most exciting ones are the *cham* dances, which take place in monastery courtyards at set times of the year. Specially trained monks dress up in rich costumes and wear huge, frightening masks. They perform a type of pantomime dance that is meant to ward off evil. Sometimes a tale is told while the dancers act out the parts. Unfortunately, these performances cannot be seen as frequently as they were in the past. Tibetan opera, called *lhamo*, is another ancient form of entertainment that hundreds of people gather to watch. Most operas are performed outside under bright canopies so that everyone can see the shows. The heartfelt singing and striking costumes make for an exciting day.

Tibetan opera, with its exquisite masks and beautiful costumes, is a lively form of entertainment.

27

Thangkas

The best-known Tibetan art form is the *thangka*. *Thangkas* are cloth banners with scenes painted on them. These rich wall hangings are draped like tapestries in temples and prayer halls. Smaller ones are placed around home altars. Like scrolls, they can be rolled up around a piece of wood for easy transport. Huge *thangkas* are brought out on special occasions. When these amazing creations are unveiled, they cover entire hillsides or monastery walls. (See the giant *thangka* on page 31.)

Before making *thangkas*, the artists meditate in order to envision holy scenes in their minds. Then they paint these scenes in great detail. After a painting is completed, strips of richly patterned silk are sewn around the edges to make a border. On most *thangkas* a main figure of Buddha is surrounded by scenes from his life. Brilliant colors and fancy curlicues are often used. As well as being beautiful works of art, *thangkas* teach people about Buddhism.

The *mandala*

The *mandala* is a special kind of design meant to represent the shape of the universe. (See the illustration on back cover.) The design is made up of overlapping geometric shapes such as triangles, squares, and circles. Sometimes a holy figure is drawn at the very center. *Mandalas* are used to help people meditate.

Sand *mandalas* are sometimes created for festival celebrations. First the sand is dyed many brilliant colors. Then a team of monks works together pouring the colored sand ever so carefully into thin lines. When completed, there are lotus flowers, little temples, miniature elephants, and tiny men—all made of sand. These masterpieces do not last long. After memorizing their beautiful creations, the monks cast them into nearby rivers.

Lifelike figures

In Tibet, statues are admired for more than their beauty. Statues of Buddha and other figures become objects of worship because they are considered holy images. They come in all sizes and varieties. Temple statues are usually made of clay covered in gold and jewels such as pearls, turquoise, and coral. These lifelike figures are dressed up in silken clothing and draped with *khata*. Some of them are hollowed out and filled with holy scrolls. For special festivals, huge butter sculptures are made by craftspeople.

An artist uses Tibetan colors as she painstakingly restores the traditional designs on a weathered building.

Molded statues

Instead of being sculpted, metal statues are made from molds. A wax figure is carefully covered in a thin coating of clay, which becomes rock hard once it has dried. Then it is heated until all the wax has melted away, leaving a hollow clay mold. The sculptor fills the mold with boiling-hot, liquid metal. After the metal has cooled and hardened, the mold is broken away to reveal a splendid statue. The surface of the sculpture is then sanded and painted.

Printing and wood carving

A traditional Tibetan book is a work of art. It has a long, thin rectangular shape. The pages are loosely stacked and sandwiched between two beautifully carved pieces of wood. The entire book is kept wrapped in a piece of embroidered cloth. Some books are written in fancy lettering; others are produced using wood blocks. The words are carved into a piece of wood, which is later covered in ink. A piece of paper is then pressed against it to produce a printed page. (See the book on page 14.)

Good vibrations

Some nomad women braid their hair into 108 strands.

To hear a group of monks chant their prayers can be a startling experience. Specially trained monks begin with a deep, pebbly, vibrating growl, but soon higher notes can be heard, as well. Each monk can sing in three-part harmony with himself! Listening to many voices chant together can make your spine tingle. For five hundred years monks have been singing in this fashion at ceremonies that sometimes last for days.

A Tibetan monk plays his horn while others chant.

Festivals

Happy New Year!

The first day of the Tibetan new year varies from year to year, but it always occurs sometime in February or early March. For the next three days Tibetans celebrate the New Year Festival called *Losar*. The first day is a religious holiday. People wake up before dawn in order to make offerings at temples or at their home altars. Prayer flags are hoisted in the breeze, and juniper branches are burned as offerings. The second day is a time of feasting and fun for everyone. Friends and family get together for big parties. On the third day they attend prayer services held on rooftops. Puffy fried pastries are prepared just for the occasion. The parties often continue for days. Yak-butter tea and barley beer flow freely. High above the ground everybody laughs, sings songs, and dances.

The Great Prayer Festival

Monlam Chemno, the Great Prayer Festival, normally begins three days after the New Year celebrations. At one time this religious festival lasted three weeks. It celebrated the time when Buddha won a great debating contest. In the past, 20,000 monks and even more pilgrims journeyed to Lhasa for this exciting festival. There were great debates by the very best scholars, horse racing, plays, and parades. Important people gave speeches, and everyone donated money to the poor. Sculptors produced giant figures made of colored butter. Today the Great Prayer Festival is a time to pray for good harvests and peace on earth.

Scrub-a-dub-dub

In the seventh month, the water in Tibet gets warm enough for swimming. Everyone goes down to the river, and the children jump into the water. Parents wash themselves, their clothes, and their children in a ritual cleansing. This community bathing party is called The Washing Festival.

Honoring Buddha

According to the Tibetan calendar, the fourth month is a very special time. On the fifteenth day of this month many centuries ago, the Buddha was born. Tibetans believe that he also had his famous vision and died on this day in later years. Long before *Saka Dawa* begins, pilgrims leave their homes so they can arrive in Lhasa during the fourth month. On the fifteenth day pilgrims and local citizens alike follow the holy route clockwise around the old section of Lhasa. The most devout pilgrims lie flat every few feet along the route, which is over six kilometers (almost four miles) long. In the streets of Lhasa people free birds and animals from their cages. This action symbolizes the Buddhist belief that living things should not be harmed.

The Summer Festival

In the summer Tibetan families get together for picnic festivals called *linka. A* few families gather at some. At others, thousands arrive from near and far, greeting old acquaintances and friends. The fields or gardens fill up with special white tents and travelers' bundles. People share tea, barley beer, scrumptious meals, and desserts of nuts, sweets, and little red cakes. No festival is complete without singing, dancing, and opera performances.

Celebrating *Lha-sol*

At many times during the year nomads perform a ceremony in which a prayer pole is raised. The participants first cover it with yak hide and then attach hundreds of prayer flags to it. Many people must pull with all their might to make the pole stand upright. Monks chant special prayers, too. Once the pole is in place, everyone circles around it in a clockwise direction, confident that the prayers on the fluttering flags are drifting up to the heavens.

Giant thangkas *such as this one are only displayed on very special occasions.*

Glossary

altitude - The height of land above sea level

artisan - A skilled craftsperson

Bon - The ancient Tibetan folk religion

Buddhism - A religion founded by Buddha, an ancient religious leader from India

chant - A type of religious singing

commune - A community in which land is held in common, and where members live and work together

culture - The customs, beliefs, and arts of a distinct group of people

debate - A formal discussion in which opinions are exchanged

embroider - To work a design into fabric with needle and yarn or thread

extended family - A family unit that includes grandparents, aunts, uncles, and cousins living together

horoscope - The forecast of a person's future according to the position of the stars and planets

incense - A substance that produces a sweet-smelling smoke when burned

Lamaist Buddhism - The form of Buddhism that developed in Tibet

lama - A leader or teacher of Lamaist Buddhism; a revered Tibetan Buddhist monk

meditate - To empty the mind of all thought in order to achieve a state of inner peace

modern convenience - Up-to-date goods and services that make life easier, such as electricity and running water

monastery - A group of buildings housing a community of monks

Mongol - A member of one of the nomadic tribes of Mongolia. Today the region known as Mongolia is part of the People's Republic of China.

monk - A male member of a religious community, which follows a set of rules or vows

Muslim - A follower of the Islamic religion

natural resources - Valuable substances that can be found in nature. Lumber, mineral deposits, and water are all natural resources.

noble - A person granted high social status because of birth

nomad - A person who travels from place to place in search of food or pastures

nuclear waste - Dangerous substances that result from the production of nuclear power or the testing of nuclear weapons, the most dangerous bombs in existence

nun - A female member of a religious community, which follows a set of rules or vows

plateau - An elevated area of relatively flat land

political turmoil - Disruption that occurs when people are unhappy with their rulers

rebellion - An uprising to overthrow an existing government or set of rulers

reincarnation - The endless cycle of birth, death, and rebirth of the same soul

ritual - A formal custom in which several steps are faithfully followed

sacrifice - An offering to a deity

temple - A sacred house of worship used by Hindus and Buddhists

tropical - Describing a hot, humid climate

Index

1 2 3 4 5 6 7 8 9 WP Printed in the U.S.A. 9 8 7 6 5 4 3 2 1 0